LAME FOR LIFE

When GOD Wrestles with Man

By Julie Anshasi

Giant Publishing Company
Lincoln, Nebraska, USA

2022 by Julie Anshasi

Published by Giant Publishing Company
Post Office Box 6455
Lincoln, NE 68506
www.giantpublishingcompany.com

Printed in the United States of America

All scripture quotations are from the King James Version of the Bible, unless otherwise noted.

Library of Congress Cataloging-in-Publication Data
Anshasi, Julie, 1963 -
Lame for Life – When GOD Wrestles with Man
        Christian Living/Julia Anshasi
    1. Christianity
    2. Christian Living
TX0009116848

ISBN 978-1-7352827-5-6

This book is dedicated to anyone who is wrestling with
God. May you win!

Books by Julia Anshasi

Broken ~ Poems from the Holy Spirit
Copyright 2017 – Winner of the 2021 Illumination Book Awards
Silver Medal

Some Things are HOT! Some Things are NOT!
Copyright 2018

Behind the Word: Bible Stories to Ignite Your Imagination
Copyright 2018

Why Did the Dinosaurs Die?
Copyright 2019

Winter in Eden
Copyright 2020 – Winner of the 2022 Illumination Book Awards
Bronze Medal

The Revelation of Jesus Christ
Copyright 2020

One Part Nonsense
Copyright 2020

Spiritual Exhaustion
Copyright 2021 - Winner of the 2022 Illumination Book Awards
Silver Medal

Forgiving Yourself
Copyright 2021

Quiet ~ A devotional
Copyright 2022

Unbearable Loneliness
Copyright 2024

7 Things God Hates
Copyright 2024

The Cult I Left
Copyright 2025

Table of Contents

Introduction

How can a man wrestle with God? And, why would he want to?

I have always been fascinated with the Biblical account of Jacob, the only man who ever wrestled with God (and lived to tell about it). In order to wrestle with God, a person must either have an enormous ego, or be in such a desperate situation that he no longer cares what happens to him. By the time Jacob had his famous wrestling match, I think he had been humbled by life's circumstances to the point that his ego was mostly gone. But he was in a desperate situation, and desperate times call for desperate measures, as the saying goes.

Jacob got what he asked for, which was God's blessing, and he paid the price for it. In this book, I lay out God's desire to bless each one of us, and explore the possibilities of what can happen when we refuse to let go of Him.

– Julia Anshasi
Author, Bible teacher, winner of multiple Christian
Illumination Book Awards

Chapter 1: Who is Jacob?

Jacob is the patriarch of the Jewish nation. Through him came the twelve tribes of Israel. He was also a con man, a trickster, and a deceiver. This was a family trait, passed down to him by his mother and his uncle.

When Jacob's father, Isaac, was old and his eyesight had faded, he asked his older son, Esau, to go hunting for him and bring him back some venison. Esau was supposed to prepare the meat and bring it to his father. Isaac then intended to bless Esau.

The family blessing is a common occurrence in the Bible. I wish more families today practiced this tradition. In Biblical times, when a father was about to die, he gathered his children around him and imparted a blessing and words of wisdom to them. Who doesn't want a blessing?

Jacob, really, really wanted a blessing. And his mother, Rebekah, really wanted him to have it. She had overheard what Isaac had told Esau to do. She then set the wheels of trickery in motion.

And Rebekah heard when Isaac spake to Esau his son. And Esau went to the field to hunt for venison, and to bring it. And Rebekah spake unto Jacob her son, saying, Behold, I heard thy father speak unto Esau thy brother, saying, Bring me venison, and make me savoury meat, that I may eat, and bless thee before the LORD *before my death. Now therefore, my son, obey my voice according to that which I command*

1

thee. Go now to the flock, and fetch me from thence two good kids of the goats; and I will make them savoury meat for thy father, such as he loveth: And thou shalt bring it to thy father, that he may eat, and that he may bless thee before his death. And Jacob said to Rebekah his mother, Behold, Esau my brother is a hairy man, and I am a smooth man: My father peradventure will feel me, and I shall seem to him as a deceiver; and I shall bring a curse upon me, and not a blessing. And his mother said unto him, Upon me be thy curse, my son: only obey my voice, and go fetch me them. Genesis 27: 5 - 13

I don't believe Jacob would have concocted this plan on his own. He had always been his mother's favorite, and she was determined that he would receive his father's blessing instead of Esau.

And Isaac loved Esau, because he did eat of his venison: but Rebekah loved Jacob. Genesis 25:28

Rebekah loved Jacob so much that she was willing to have a curse put upon her in order for her son to receive a stolen blessing! But Rebekah didn't have the authority to dictate to God who He should bless and who He should curse. This becomes evident as we study the life of Jacob.

Jacob obeyed his mother, and brought her the goat kids from their flock. She prepared the meat, and prepared her son. Jacob had to dress up in Esau's clothing and put the goats' skins on his neck and the backs of his hands, in order to deceive his own father.

Isaac, not being a fool, did suspect that something was amiss when Jacob brought him the food. He recognized the voice that spoke to him as Jacob's voice, but when he touched his son, he felt Esau's hairy skin, and smelled the outdoorsy smell of his clothes.

And he said, Art thou my very son Esau? And (Jacob) said, I am. And he said, Bring it near to me, and I will eat of my son's venison, that my soul may bless thee. And he brought it near to him, and he did eat: and he brought him wine and he drank. And his father Isaac said unto him, Come near now, and kiss me, my son. And he came near, and kissed him: and he smelled the smell of his raiment, and blessed him, and said, See, the smell of my son is as the smell of a field which the LORD hath blessed: Therefore God give thee of the dew of heaven, and the fatness of the earth, and plenty of corn and wine: Let people serve thee, and nations bow down to thee: be lord over thy brethren, and let thy mother's sons bow down to thee: cursed be every one that curseth thee, and blessed be he that blesseth thee. And it came to pass, as soon as Isaac had made an end of blessing Jacob, and Jacob was yet scarce gone out from the presence of Isaac his father, that Esau his brother came in from his hunting. Genesis 27: 24 - 30

Uh oh.

There is little doubt that Jacob knew that what he had done was wrong, wrong, wrong. Deception and trickery are never right! But this wasn't the first time Jacob had conned someone.

And Jacob sod pottage: and Esau came from the field, and he was faint: And Esau said to Jacob, Feed me, I pray thee, with that same red pottage; for I am faint: therefore was his name called Edom. And Jacob said, Sell me this day thy birthright. And Esau said, Behold, I am at the point to die: and what profit shall this birthright do to me? And Jacob said, Swear to me this day; and he sware unto him: and he sold his birthright unto Jacob. Then Jacob gave Esau bread and pottage of lentiles; and he did eat and drink, and rose up, and went his way: thus Esau despised his birthright. Genesis 25: 29 - 34

I think Esau was the kind of person who lived for the moment. He was hungry after hunting all day, he wanted food, he demanded that his brother give him some of the food that he was cooking, and he really thought no further beyond the meal that he was about to get. Most of us can skip a meal (or two) and not die! If Esau had taken the time to think it through, he would have realized that he was throwing away his inheritance for a bowl of lentils. That is not an even trade! But Jacob had carefully calculated the situation ahead of time. He took advantage of Esau's hunger and impetuous nature, and used them to his full advantage.

It's likely that this encounter with his brother strengthened Jacob's natural tendency to con others. It planted even more firmly in Jacob's heart the seeds of future trickery.

So, Jacob tricked his father into blessing him instead of Esau. After Jacob escaped out of the room with his freshly-stolen blessing, Esau came in.

And (Esau) also had made savoury meat, and brought it unto his father, and said unto his father, Let my father arise, and eat of his son's venison, that thy soul may bless me. And Isaac his father said unto him, Who art thou? And he said, I am thy son, thy firstborn Esau. And Isaac trembled very exceedingly, and said, Who? where is he that hath taken venison, and brought it me, and I have eaten of all before thou camest, and have blessed him? yea, and he shall be blessed. And when Esau heard the words of his father, he cried with a great and exceeding bitter cry, and said unto his father, Bless me, even me also, O my father. And he said, Thy brother came with subtilty, and hath taken away thy blessing. And he said, Is not he rightly named Jacob? for he hath supplanted me these two times: he took away my birthright; and, behold, now he hath taken away my blessing. And he said, Hast thou not reserved a blessing for me? And Isaac answered and said unto Esau, Behold, I have made him thy lord, and all his brethren have I given to him for servants; and with corn and wine have I sustained him: and what shall I do now unto thee, my son? And Esau said unto his father, Hast thou but one blessing, my father? bless me, even me also, O my father. And Esau lifted up his voice, and wept. Genesis 27: 31 - 38

5

Jacob's deception planted other seeds as well – in Esau's heart.

And Esau hated Jacob because of the blessing wherewith his father blessed him: and Esau said in his heart, The days of mourning for my father are at hand; then will I slay my brother Jacob. Genesis 27:41

Did Rebekah stop to think through her actions? Surely, she should have known that pitting one child against another could not possibly end well.

And these words of Esau her elder son were told to Rebekah: and she sent and called Jacob her younger son, and said unto him, Behold, thy brother Esau, as touching thee, doth comfort himself, purposing to kill thee. Now therefore, my son, obey my voice; arise, flee thou to Laban my brother to Haran; And tarry with him a few days, until thy brother's fury turn away; Until thy brother's anger turn away from thee, and he forget that which thou hast done to him: then I will send, and fetch thee from thence: why should I be deprived also of you both in one day? Genesis 27: 42 - 45

Rebekah's scheme could not have turned out worse for her. She urged her son to run and hide in her brother's house, telling him she would send for him to come back in "a few days," but in reality, she never saw Jacob again. He fled to his uncle's house, stayed there for years, and Rebekah died before he came back.

Jacob's upbringing is a picture of a family in turmoil. Favoritism, lies, trickery, murder, and a lot of tears. What a sad situation.

What about Esau?

And Esau was forty years old when he took to wife Judith the daughter of Beeri the Hittite, and Bashemath the daughter of Elon the Hittite: Which were a grief of mind unto Isaac and to Rebekah. Genesis 26: 34 – 35

Esau had married two wives before his brother left. His parents did not approve of his wives. In keeping with his instant gratification personality, I doubt if he had given much thought ahead of time to his parents' approval or disapproval of his choices. But the incident of Jacob stealing his blessing caused him to begin to think twice.

And Isaac sent away Jacob: and he went to Padanaram unto Laban, son of Bethuel the Syrian, the brother of Rebekah, Jacob's and Esau's mother. When Esau saw that Isaac had blessed Jacob, and sent him away to Padanaram, to take him a wife from thence; and that as he blessed him he gave him a charge, saying, Thou shalt not take a wife of the daughters of Canaan; And that Jacob obeyed his father and his mother, and was gone to Padanaram; And Esau seeing that the daughters of Canaan pleased not Isaac his father; Then went Esau unto Ishmael, and took unto the wives which he had Mahalath the daughter of

Ishmael Abraham's son, the sister of Nebajoth, to be his wife. Genesis 28: 5 – 9

Now Esau had three wives. The first two hadn't pleased his parents, so he added Mahalath, his uncle's daughter.

It's hard to say for sure what Esau's mindset was. Perhaps he thought that he had lost his birthright, lost his blessing, and lost the favor of his parents, so he had better do something to try to set things right. We do know that his anger toward Jacob eventually cooled, as we will see later.

Chapter 2: The trickster is tricked

Jacob fled to Padanaram, to his uncle Laban's house. His mother had told him to stay for a few days, until Esau's desire to kill him had faded. He ended up staying for more than twenty years.

I do firmly believe that our God has a sense of humor.

And Jacob went out from Beersheba, and went toward Haran. And he lighted upon a certain place, and tarried there all night, because the sun was set; and he took of the stones of that place, and put them for his pillows, and lay down in that place to sleep. And he dreamed, and behold a ladder set up on the earth, and the top of it reached to heaven: and behold the angels of God ascending and descending on it. And, behold, the LORD stood above it, and said, I am the LORD God of Abraham thy father, and the God of Isaac: the land whereon thou liest, to thee will I give it, and to thy seed; And thy seed shall be as the dust of the earth, and thou shalt spread abroad to the west, and to the east, and to the north, and to the south: and in thee and in thy seed shall all the families of the earth be blessed. And, behold, I am with thee, and will keep thee in all places whither thou goest, and will bring thee again into this land; for I will not leave thee, until I have done that which I have spoken to thee of. Genesis 28: 10 - 15

What a blessing! God truly loved Jacob, in spite of his deceitful ways, and He appeared to Jacob at Bethel and told him so.

...and in thy seed shall all the families of the earth be blessed...

Where have we seen this promise before?

And I will bless them that bless thee, and curse him that curseth thee: and in thee shall all families of the earth be blessed. Genesis 12:3

This was God's promise to Abraham, Jacob's grandfather.

Jacob was blessed; there's no doubt about it.

And Jacob awaked out of his sleep, and he said, Surely the LORD is in this place; and I knew it not. And he was afraid, and said, How dreadful is this place! this is none other but the house of God, and this is the gate of heaven. And Jacob rose up early in the morning, and took the stone that he had put for his pillows, and set it up for a pillar, and poured oil upon the top of it. And he called the name of that place Bethel: but the name of that city was called Luz at the first. And Jacob vowed a vow, saying, If God will be with me, and will keep me in this way that I go, and will give me bread to eat, and raiment to put on, So that I come again to my father's house in peace; then shall the LORD be my God: And this stone, which I have set for a pillar, shall be God's house: and of all that thou shalt give me I will surely give the tenth unto thee. Genesis 28: 16 – 22

Jacob had the good sense to recognize God's blessing on his life. He vowed to give God ten percent of all his future wealth.

Jacob made his way to his uncle Laban's house. He stopped to rest near a well. His cousin, Rachel, came to water her father's sheep.

For Jacob, it was love at first sight. Rachel brought him home, introduced him to her parents, and they had a grand old family reunion. Little did Jacob know that he had met his match in the form of Laban, his uncle, who may well have been the greatest con man of that day.

After staying with Laban as an honored guest for a month, Laban suddenly introduced a new condition on Jacob's visit.

And Laban said unto Jacob, Because thou art my brother, shouldest thou therefore serve me for nought? tell me, what shall thy wages be? And Laban had two daughters: the name of the elder was Leah, and the name of the younger was Rachel. Leah was tender eyed; but Rachel was beautiful and well favoured. And Jacob loved Rachel; and said, I will serve thee seven years for Rachel thy younger daughter. And Laban said, It is better that I give her to thee, than that I should give her to another man: abide with me. Genesis 29: 15 – 19

The Bible doesn't record that Jacob did any work for Laban during the first month he stayed with him.

Apparently, Laban was getting tired of this charming young man, hanging around and eating his food. So, he decided to make an employment contract with him. Jacob was so in love with Rachel that he didn't even stop to question this. He could have simply said, "You know, Uncle Laban, my parents sent me here with specific instructions that I was to marry one of your daughters. Nobody said anything about working for you!" But, he didn't.

And Jacob served seven years for Rachel; and they seemed unto him but a few days, for the love he had to her. And Jacob said unto Laban, Give me my wife, for my days are fulfilled, that I may go in unto her. And Laban gathered together all the men of the place, and made a feast. And it came to pass in the evening, that he took Leah his daughter, and brought her to him; and he went in unto her. And Laban gave unto his daughter Leah Zilpah his maid for an handmaid. And it came to pass, that in the morning, behold, it was Leah: and he said to Laban, What is this thou hast done unto me? did not I serve with thee for Rachel? wherefore then hast thou beguiled me? Genesis 29: 20 - 25

Yes, the trickster had been tricked. And it really was a very dirty trick.

In Biblical times, a woman wore a covering over her face during her wedding ceremony. Jacob thought he was marrying Rachel, the love of his life, but his father-in-law had substituted Leah, and Jacob slept with her that night, not knowing what had happened.

And Laban said, It must not be so done in our country, to give the younger before the firstborn. Fulfil her week, and we will give thee this also for the service which thou shalt serve with me yet seven other years. And Jacob did so, and fulfilled her week: and he gave him Rachel his daughter to wife also. And Laban gave to Rachel his daughter Bilhah his handmaid to be her maid. And he went in also unto Rachel, and he loved also Rachel more than Leah, and served with him yet seven other years. Genesis 29: 26 – 30

So now, Jacob had worked for his father-in-law for a total of twenty-one years. A period of seven years is referred to as a week in these passages. He had two wives – one that he loved, and one that he felt a lot of resentment toward.

And when the LORD saw that Leah was hated, he opened her womb: but Rachel was barren. Genesis 29: 31

I believe that Jacob was beginning to see the consequences of his prior deception of his brother and father. In the world we say, "What goes around, comes around." The Bible says:

Be not deceived; God is not mocked: for whatsoever a man soweth, that shall he also reap. Galatians 6:7

Nobody ever plants tomatoes and harvests squash. Nobody ever lives a life of deceiving others, and does not get deceived in return.

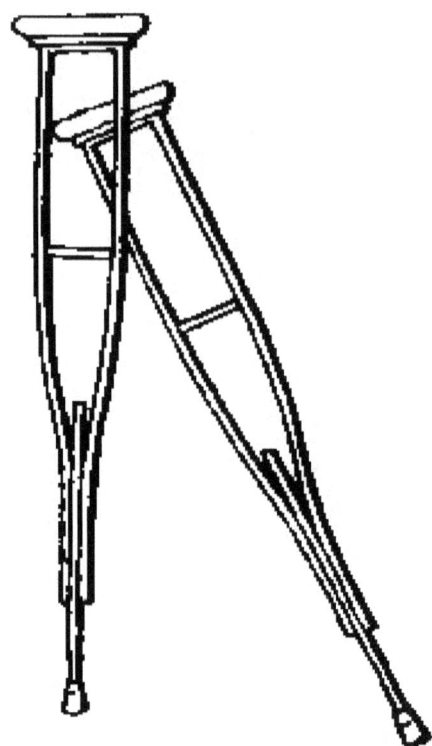

Chapter 3: A family wrestling match

And when Rachel saw that she bare Jacob no children, Rachel envied her sister; and said unto Jacob, Give me children, or else I die. And Jacob's anger was kindled against Rachel: and he said, Am I in God's stead, who hath withheld from thee the fruit of the womb? Genesis 30: 1 - 2

I think Jacob was nearing the end of his rope. He lashed out at his beloved wife, Rachel, and told her that he wasn't God, and that he had no control over whether she got pregnant or not. Although I'm sure that he had some love for the children that Leah had borne him, there was probably at least some pain in his heart in knowing that his beloved was barren.

In keeping with the custom of the day, both Leah and Rachel gave their handmaids to Jacob as concubines. Zilpah and Bilhah were their names, and they also bore children by Jacob.

And (Rachel) said, Behold my maid Bilhah, go in unto her; and she shall bear upon my knees, that I may also have children by her. And she gave him Bilhah her handmaid to wife: and Jacob went in unto her. And Bilhah conceived, and bare Jacob a son. And Rachel said, God hath judged me, and hath also heard my voice, and hath given me a son: therefore called she his name Dan. And Bilhah Rachel's maid conceived again, and bare Jacob a second son. And Rachel said, With great wrestlings have I wrestled with my sister, and I have prevailed: and she called his name Naphtali. Genesis 30: 3 - 8

Naphtali means "my wrestling," or, "to twist or be cunning."

Jacob's family of origin was marked by deceit, and his new family with his many wives and children (not to mention his father-in-law) was no different. Rachel most definitely saw herself in a competition with her sister, and she was determined to win.

But Leah was also determined.

When Leah saw that she had left bearing, she took Zilpah her maid, and gave her Jacob to wife. And Zilpah Leah's maid bare Jacob a son. And Leah said, A troop cometh: and she called his name Gad. And Zilpah Leah's maid bare Jacob a second son. And Leah said, Happy am I, for the daughters will call me blessed: and she called his name Asher. And Reuben went in the days of wheat harvest, and found mandrakes in the field, and brought them unto his mother Leah. Then Rachel said to Leah, Give me, I pray thee, of thy son's mandrakes. And she said unto her, Is it a small matter that thou hast taken my husband? and wouldest thou take away my son's mandrakes also? And Rachel said, Therefore he shall lie with thee to night for thy son's mandrakes. And Jacob came out of the field in the evening, and Leah went out to meet him, and said, Thou must come in unto me; for surely I have hired thee with my son's mandrakes. And he lay with her that night. Genesis 30: 9 – 16

There is a lot to absorb in these few verses. Reuben, Leah's first son with Jacob, brought his mother mandrakes, which in ancient times were thought to help a woman conceive. Rachel desperately wanted those mandrakes! Leah was angry with Rachel and accused her of stealing her husband, and then trying to steal her mandrakes.

It's interesting that Leah saw the situation that way. Certainly, she knew of the deception perpetrated by her father on her wedding night. Yet, she saw herself as Jacob's rightful wife, and Rachel as the imposter.

In this family, it seems that the women controlled the sleeping arrangements, because Rachel told her sister that Jacob would sleep with Leah that night, if Leah gave Rachel the mandrakes.

I can't help but feel a little sorry for Jacob, stuck in the middle between two wrestling and squabbling sisters.

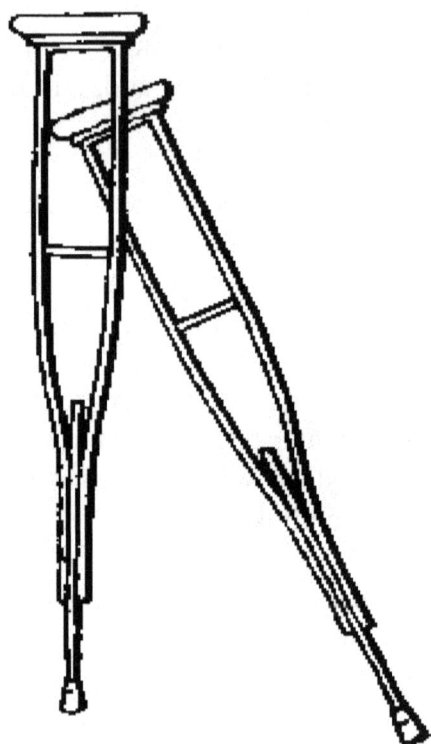

Chapter 4: Journey to a blessing

*And God remembered Rachel, and God hearkened to her, and opened her womb. And she conceived, and bare a son; and said, God hath taken away my reproach: And she called his name Joseph; and said, The L*ORD *shall add to me another son. And it came to pass, when Rachel had born Joseph, that Jacob said unto Laban, Send me away, that I may go unto mine own place, and to my country. Give me my wives and my children, for whom I have served thee, and let me go: for thou knowest my service which I have done thee.* Genesis 30: 22 - 26

Jacob, the trickster, had had enough of his tricky father-in-law. He was ready to go back to his parents' home. The Bible does not record Rebekah's death, but from the context of Jacob's journey back, we can conclude that she was no longer living by the time he made the decision to return.

Laban, ever the deal-maker, wanted to make another deal with Jacob. He really didn't want Jacob to leave, and he thought he should try to make the idea of staying as appealing as possible.

*And Laban said unto him, I pray thee, if I have found favour in thine eyes, tarry: for I have learned by experience that the L*ORD *hath blessed me for thy sake.* Genesis 30: 27

Laban was no fool. He knew that he had started out with little, and since Jacob had been living with him, everything he owned had multiplied.

And he said, Appoint me thy wages, and I will give it.
Genesis 30:28

In other words, "Jacob, name your salary, and I will pay you that."

And he said unto him, Thou knowest how I have served thee, and how thy cattle was with me. For it was little which thou hadst before I came, and it is now increased unto a multitude; and the LORD hath blessed thee since my coming: and now when shall I provide for mine own house also? And he said, What shall I give thee? And Jacob said, Thou shalt not give me any thing: if thou wilt do this thing for me, I will again feed and keep thy flock. I will pass through all thy flock to day, removing from thence all the speckled and spotted cattle, and all the brown cattle among the sheep, and the spotted and speckled among the goats: and of such shall be my hire. So shall my righteousness answer for me in time to come, when it shall come for my hire before thy face: every one that is not speckled and spotted among the goats, and brown among the sheep, that shall be counted stolen with me. And Laban said, Behold, I would it might be according to thy word.
Genesis 30: 29 – 34

Jacob had a plan. He told his father-in-law that he wanted nothing from him except the animals that were spotted or brown. He would go through Laban's flocks, pick out all the spotted and brown ones, separate them from the plain white ones, and keep the spotted and brown ones for himself. Later, if Laban inspected any of Jacob's animals that had been separated from Laban's, and found any white ones among them, he would know that Jacob had stolen the white ones. Laban appeared to agree to this plan, but he had his own devious plan. Before Jacob could do anything, Laban went through his own flocks and removed all of the spotted and brown animals, put his sons in charge of them, and he and his sons traveled three days' journey away, taking those animals with them.

Now Jacob was left with only the white animals, which he and Laban had agreed would belong to Laban.

Once again, Jacob had been tricked by Laban. He had to count on God to fight for him in this situation. Jacob knew that God had blessed Laban's herds and caused them to multiply, and he asked God to now bless his own herds.

Now Jacob took for himself rods of green poplar and of the almond and chestnut trees, peeled white strips in them, and exposed the white which was in the rods. And the rods which he had peeled, he set before the flocks in the gutters, in the watering troughs where the flocks came to drink, so that they should conceive when they came to drink. So the flocks conceived before the rods, and the flocks brought forth streaked, speckled, and spotted. Then Jacob separated the lambs, and made the flocks face toward the streaked and all the brown in the flock of Laban; but he put his own flocks by themselves and did not put them with Laban's flock. And it came to pass, whenever the stronger livestock conceived, that Jacob placed the rods before the eyes of the livestock in the gutters, that they might conceive among the rods. But when the flocks were feeble, he did not put them in; so the feebler were Laban's and the stronger Jacob's. Thus the man became exceedingly prosperous, and had large flocks, female and male servants, and camels and donkeys. Genesis 30: 37 – 43, New King James Version

This is such a funny story. From the human perspective, peeling strips of bark off of tree branches and putting them in front of mating animals not only does not help them to conceive, it also does not ensure that their offspring will be spotted or brown. But God most certainly has a sense of humor! Laban thought he could cheat Jacob out of the wage he had asked for (spotted and brown animals), but God made sure that the only animals remaining in Jacob's care – the white ones – gave birth to only spotted and brown offspring. He used stripped tree branches to do it.

If God can part the Red Sea, turn water into wine, rain bread from heaven and make the blind see, He most certainly can use tree branches to help animals conceive whatever color of young He wants them to conceive. He's a God of miracles, after all.

So now, Jacob was very wealthy, and Laban's wealth was rapidly dwindling.

As could be expected, Laban was none too happy with Jacob over this turn of events.

And Jacob beheld the countenance of Laban, and, behold, it was not toward him as before. And the LORD said unto Jacob, Return unto the land of thy fathers, and to thy kindred; and I will be with thee. Genesis 31: 2 - 3

Jacob had a conference with his wives. They were well aware of their father's shady dealings, and they were none too happy with him, either.

And Rachel and Leah answered and said unto him, Is there yet any portion or inheritance for us in our father's house? Are we not counted of him strangers? for he hath sold us, and hath quite devoured also our money. For all the riches which God hath taken from our father, that is ours, and our children's: now then, whatsoever God hath said unto thee, do. Genesis 31: 14 - 16

For the second time, Jacob made the decision to leave his father-in-law, and this time, he actually left.

Then Jacob rose up, and set his sons and his wives upon camels; And he carried away all his cattle, and all his goods which he had gotten, the cattle of his getting, which he had gotten in Padanaram, for to go to Isaac his father in the land of Canaan. Genesis 31: 17 – 18

It's ironic that people who spend their lives tricking others get really upset when they themselves are tricked.

Laban got really upset when Jacob left. There were probably several reasons for this. Jacob left without saying goodbye, while Laban was away shearing his sheep. Jacob took with him all of his rightfully-owned herds and flocks of animals, which diminished Laban's estate even further. And, Laban knew that Jacob carried enormous blessings with him, so, goodbye to Jacob meant goodbye to Laban's blessings, even if those blessings were second-hand.

Laban pursued after Jacob and caught up with him, and the two of them had it out.

And Laban said to Jacob, What hast thou done, that thou hast stolen away unawares to me, and carried away my daughters, as captives taken with the sword? Wherefore didst thou flee away secretly, and steal away from me; and didst not tell me, that I might have sent thee away with mirth, and with songs, with tabret, and with harp? And hast not suffered me to kiss my sons and my daughters? thou hast now done foolishly in so doing. Genesis 31: 26 - 28

Laban accused Jacob of stealing his gods (Rachel was the actual thief). This set Jacob off, and the two of them really went at it. Laban proved himself to be a very stubborn man by what he said to Jacob.

And Laban answered and said unto Jacob, These daughters are my daughters, and these children are my children, and these cattle are my cattle, and all that thou seest is mine: and what can I do this day unto these my daughters, or unto their children which they have born? Genesis 31: 43

Laban wrongly claimed everything that was Jacob's as his own. But he knew there was nothing he could do to Jacob, because God had warned him (Genesis 31: 29).

Jacob and Laban made an uneasy truce with one another. Laban camped with them for the night, then got up in the morning and went back to his home (Genesis 31: 44 – 55).

Jacob, the junior con artist, was finally free of Laban, the senior con artist.

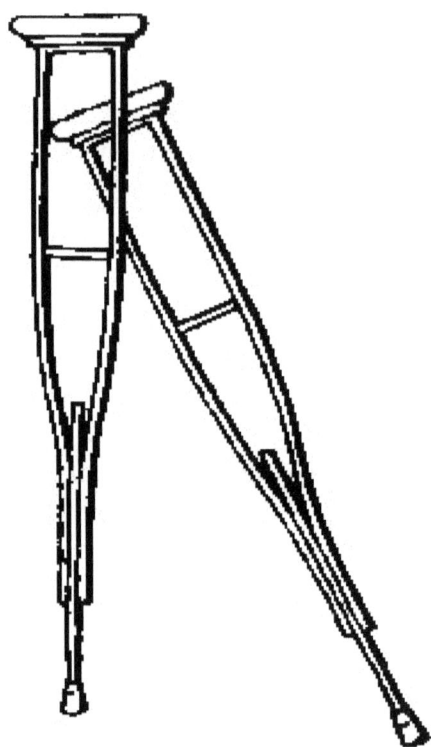

Chapter 5: The identification

Remember Esau?

Jacob's brother, the last time we read about him, had been planning to kill Jacob because of all his trickery. I believe this was very much at the forefront of Jacob's mind, as he made his way back to his home country.

And the LORD said unto Jacob, Return unto the land of thy fathers, and to thy kindred; and I will be with thee. Genesis 31: 3

And Jacob went on his way, and the angels of God met him. And when Jacob saw them, he said, This is God's host: and he called the name of that place Mahanaim (two camps). Genesis 32: 1 - 2

It didn't take long for God to show Jacob that He was, indeed, with him. He sent angels to meet him!

And Jacob sent messengers before him to Esau his brother unto the land of Seir, the country of Edom. And he commanded them, saying, Thus shall ye speak unto my lord Esau; Thy servant Jacob saith thus, I have sojourned with Laban, and stayed there until now: And I have oxen, and asses, flocks, and menservants, and womenservants: and I have sent to tell my lord, that I may find grace in thy sight. And the messengers returned to Jacob, saying, We came to thy brother Esau, and also he cometh to meet thee, and four hundred men with him. Genesis 32: 3 – 6

As quickly as Jacob's faith rose at the appearance of the angels, his faith disappeared at the news that Esau was coming to meet him with four hundred men.

Then Jacob was greatly afraid and distressed: and he divided the people that was with him, and the flocks, and herds, and the camels, into two bands; And said, If Esau come to the one company, and smite it, then the other company which is left shall escape. And Jacob said, O God of my father Abraham, and God of my father Isaac, the LORD which saidst unto me, Return unto thy country, and to thy kindred, and I will deal well with thee: I am not worthy of the least of all the mercies, and of all the truth, which thou hast shewed unto thy servant; for with my staff I passed over this Jordan; and now I am become two bands. Deliver me, I pray thee, from the hand of my brother, from the hand of Esau: for I fear him, lest he will come and smite me, and the mother with the children. Genesis 32: 7 - 11

Jacob had learned a thing or two while he lived with Laban. He had learned that if you trick others, you yourself will be tricked. He probably thought that his time was up. Esau had been waiting patiently all these years, and now, Jacob had made it easy for him by coming back. He reminded God that He had told him that He would be with him, if he went back home.

Jacob decided that a little bribery wouldn't hurt. So, he gathered up a large number of his animals and sent them on ahead of him with his servants. He told them:

And say ye moreover, Behold, thy servant Jacob is behind us. For he said, I will appease him with the present that goeth before me, and afterward I will see his face; peradventure he will accept of me. So went the present over before him: and himself lodged that night in the company. Genesis 32: 20 - 21

Jacob spent a sleepless night.

Have you ever wrestled with your conscience? Have you ever been kept awake by the thought, "What if...?" I'm quite sure that Jacob began mentally rehearsing all of his past misdeeds, and as always, was trying to figure out on his own how to get out of the mess he thought he was about to walk into.

And he rose up that night, and took his two wives, and his two womenservants, and his eleven sons, and passed over the ford Jabbok. And he took them, and sent them over the brook, and sent over that he had. Genesis 32: 22 - 23

Jacob's solution to his sleeplessness was to wake everybody else up, and send them on ahead of him. I think he knew something big was about to happen.

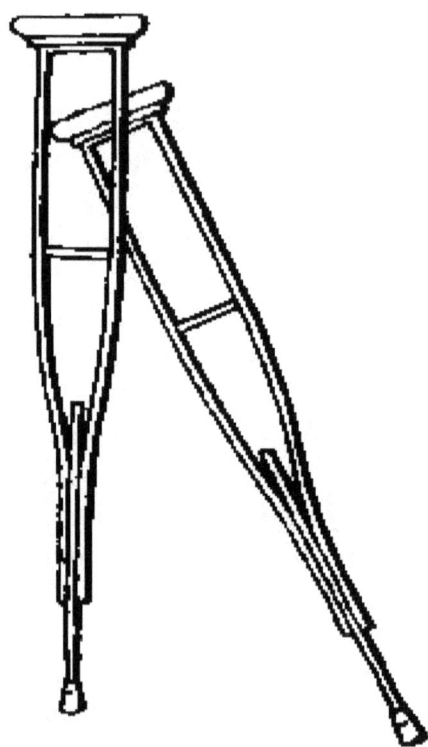

Chapter 6: The match

Jacob was a man who'd had many encounters with God. When he first left home, fleeing from his murderous brother, God spoke to him at Bethel. He saw a vision of angels going up and down a ladder between heaven and earth. He built a pillar to mark the spot, and called the place Bethel, which means "house of God." We read about this in Chapter 2 (Genesis 28: 10 – 22).

While living with his uncle Laban, he witnessed with his own eyes the power of God, when He supernaturally enabled the animals to conceive spotted and brown offspring (Genesis 30: 37 – 39). We read about this in Chapter 4.

And, when he finally left Laban's house and headed back to his father's house, angels met him on the way.

And Jacob went on his way, and the angels of God met him. And when Jacob saw them, he said, This is God's host: and he called the name of that place Mahanaim. Genesis 32: 1 - 2

Jacob was not a stranger to heavenly encounters. But the one he was about to have was most certainly the strangest encounter yet.

And he rose up that night, and took his two wives, and his two womenservants, and his eleven sons, and passed over the ford Jabbok. And he took them, and sent them over the brook, and sent over that he had. Genesis 32: 22 - 23

Jacob's courage had disappeared when he learned that his brother was on his way to meet him, and was bringing four hundred men with him. He couldn't sleep, got up in the middle of the night, and sent his wives, children, and animals on ahead of him.

In my book, *"Forgiving Yourself"* (Copyright 2021, Giant Publishing Company), I touched on Jacob's state of mind after he sent his entourage on ahead. I believe that Jacob was beginning to realize the consequences of living a life of deceit, and he knew that he needed God's forgiveness.

And Jacob was left alone; and there wrestled a man with him until the breaking of the day. Genesis 32: 24

This verse jumps off the pages of scripture with no warning. Did God tell Jacob that this was about to happen, and so he sent everyone else on ahead? Or did it happen because Jacob was now finally alone?

Where did this man come from? Who was he? And why did he wrestle with Jacob?

Chapter 7: Perseverance

And when he saw that he prevailed not against him…
Genesis 32: 25a

You have to read this part of the verse carefully to understand which "he" and "him" the Bible is referring to.   The man that Jacob was wrestling with wasn't winning, to put it bluntly.

As we continue reading the scripture, it becomes clear who the man was.   God Himself was wrestling with Jacob - a preincarnate visitation by Jesus Christ.

This makes sense.   God is a spirit.   God appeared to Jacob in the form of a human being – Jesus Christ – and wrestled with him.

Why couldn't God prevail against Jacob?   Why wasn't this wrestling match over before it started?   The answer is found in other scriptures.

And he spake a parable unto them to this end, that men ought always to pray, and not to faint; Saying, There was in a city a judge, which feared not God, neither regarded man: And there was a widow in that city; and she came unto him, saying, Avenge me of mine adversary.   And he would not for a while: but afterward he said within himself, Though I fear not God, nor regard man; Yet because this widow troubleth me, I will avenge her, lest by her continual coming she weary me.   And the Lord said, Hear what the unjust judge saith.   And shall not God avenge his own elect, which cry day and night unto him, though he bear long with them? Luke 18: 1 – 7

One of the many mysteries of God is that He expects you and me to ask Him, over and over, for what we want.

As a child growing up, I heard a preacher say that if you ask God for the same thing more than once, it means you have no faith, and your continual asking is very displeasing to God. But the parable that Jesus told above disproves that idea.

The widow in this parable kept asking the judge, day after day, for him to settle her case. He finally did. The implication of this parable is that if she had not asked him, over and over, he would not have done it. Jesus told this parable to illustrate how vital perseverance is in our walk with Him.

Here is another example of someone in the scripture who wouldn't take no for an answer.

Then Jesus went thence, and departed into the coasts of Tyre and Sidon. And, behold, a woman of Canaan came out of the same coasts, and cried unto him, saying, Have mercy on me, O Lord, thou son of David; my daughter is grievously vexed with a devil. But he answered her not a word. And his disciples came and besought him, saying, Send her away; for she crieth after us. But he answered and said, I am not sent but unto the lost sheep of the house of Israel. Then came she and worshipped him, saying, Lord, help me. But he answered and said, It is not meet to take the children's bread, and to cast it to dogs. And she said, Truth, Lord: yet the dogs eat of the crumbs which fall from their masters' table. Then Jesus answered and said unto her, O woman, great is thy faith: be it unto thee even as thou wilt. And her daughter was made whole from that very hour. Matthew 15: 21 – 28

This woman was so desperate for Jesus to heal her daughter that she was willing to be insulted by Him. Try calling someone a dog and see how he or she reacts to you! On second thought, don't try it!

God tests our faith. This is not for His benefit, but for ours. God knows before we do or say anything, what we are going to do or say. But when He tests our faith, and we pass the test, we emerge with a new understanding of who we are dealing with. This is always a very humbling and immensely growing experience.

And it came to pass after these things, that God did tempt Abraham, and said unto him, Abraham: and he said, Behold, here I am. And he said, Take now thy son, thine only son Isaac, whom thou lovest, and get thee into the land of Moriah; and offer him there for a burnt offering upon one of the mountains which I will tell thee of. Genesis 22: 1 - 2

The King James version of the Bible translates the word "test" as "tempt" in verse one. This was truly a test for Abraham. God knew what Abraham would do, but He wanted Abraham to know what Abraham would do!

And Abraham stretched forth his hand, and took the knife to slay his son. And the angel of the LORD called unto him out of heaven, and said, Abraham, Abraham: and he said, Here am I. And he said, Lay not thine hand upon the lad, neither do thou any thing unto him: for now I know that thou fearest God, seeing thou hast not withheld thy son, thine only son from me. Genesis 22: 10 - 12

God knew before Abraham ever lifted the knife that he was willing to sacrifice his own son. He said "now I know" so that Abraham would see what was in his own heart, and so that Abraham would know that God was able to deliver him out of any situation.

How did Abraham feel when he realized he would not have to kill his beloved son, after all? I tell you that he felt gratitude beyond anything he had felt before, and his relationship with his Father God was strengthened beyond any measure it had been measured by before.

God wants obedience from us. Sometimes what He is asking us to do is more than a human being can bear.

And he went a little farther, and fell on his face, and prayed, saying, O my Father, if it be possible, let this cup pass from me: nevertheless not as I will, but as thou wilt. Matthew 26: 39

Jesus was willing to go to the cross, because His Father God asked Him to. He asked His Father to relieve Him of this responsibility, if it were at all possible to do so, but in the end He agreed to be beaten, tortured, nailed to a cross, and executed like a criminal, for a crime He didn't commit.

In Daniel chapter 3, we read the account of Shadrach, Meshach, and Abednego, who refused to worship a golden statue. King Nebuchadnezzar had made a law that everyone had to bow down and worship this huge statue of himself, whenever they heard the worship music playing. Nebuchadnezzar was a massive egomaniac, and quite mentally ill, in my opinion.

Nebuchadnezzar spake and said unto them, Is it true, O Shadrach, Meshach, and Abednego, do not ye serve my gods, nor worship the golden image which I have set up? Now if ye be ready that at what time ye hear the sound of the cornet, flute, harp, sackbut, psaltery, and dulcimer, and all kinds of musick, ye fall down and worship the image which I have made; well: but if ye worship not, ye shall be cast the same hour into the midst of a burning fiery furnace; and who is that God that shall deliver you out of my hands? Shadrach, Meshach, and Abednego, answered and said to the king, O Nebuchadnezzar, we are not careful to answer thee in this matter. If it be so, our God whom we serve is able to deliver us from the burning fiery furnace, and he will deliver us out of thine hand, O king. But if not, be it known unto thee, O king, that we will not serve thy gods, nor worship the golden image which thou hast set up. Daniel 3: 14 - 18

Nebuchadnezzar actually believed that God could not save these three men from death by fire. He actually believed that he had more power than God.

But Shadrach, Meshach, and Abednego were not going to worship the golden statue of an egomaniacal king, even if it meant that they would die.

Then these men were bound in their coats, their hosen, and their hats, and their other garments, and were cast into the midst of the burning fiery furnace. Therefore because the king's commandment was urgent, and the furnace exceeding hot, the flames of the fire slew those men that took up Shadrach, Meshach, and Abednego. And these three men, Shadrach, Meshach, and Abednego, fell down bound into the midst of the burning fiery furnace. Then Nebuchadnezzar the king was astonished, and rose up in haste, and spake, and said unto his counsellors, Did not we cast three men bound into the midst of the fire? They answered and said unto the king, True, O king. He answered and said, Lo, I see four men loose, walking in the midst of the fire, and they have no hurt; and the form of the fourth is like the Son of God. Then Nebuchadnezzar came near to the mouth of the burning fiery furnace, and spake, and said, Shadrach, Meshach, and Abednego, ye servants of the most high God, come forth, and come hither. Then Shadrach, Meshach, and Abednego, came forth of the midst of the fire. Daniel 3: 21 - 26

I suspect the king's massive ego was somewhat deflated by this incident.

38

Why does God want us to persevere in Him? Even the mother of Jesus had to persevere, and the result was the first recorded miracle that Jesus did.

And when they wanted wine, the mother of Jesus saith unto him, They have no wine. Jesus saith unto her, Woman, what have I to do with thee? mine hour is not yet come. His mother saith unto the servants, Whatsoever he saith unto you, do it. John 2: 3 – 5

Jesus plainly told His mother that it wasn't yet time for Him to do a miracle, yet, because she persevered, He turned water into wine.

Jesus saith unto them, Fill the waterpots with water. And they filled them up to the brim. And he saith unto them, Draw out now, and bear unto the governor of the feast. And they bare it. When the ruler of the feast had tasted the water that was made wine, and knew not whence it was: (but the servants which drew the water knew;) the governor of the feast called the bridegroom, And saith unto him, Every man at the beginning doth set forth good wine; and when men have well drunk, then that which is worse: but thou hast kept the good wine until now. This beginning of miracles did Jesus in Cana of Galilee, and manifested forth his glory; and his disciples believed on him. John 2: 7 – 11

Jesus prayed a magnificent prayer in John chapter 17. He was praying for His disciples, and all believers, when He said this:

That they all may be one; as thou, Father, art in me, and I in thee, that they also may be one in us: that the world may believe that thou hast sent me. John 17: 21

A very interesting thing to note about Jesus' prayer is this: it hasn't yet been fulfilled! Are believers all over the world now one in God, and one in Jesus Christ? Of course, the answer is no. Think about that for a moment. A prayer prayed by the Son of God, two thousand years ago, has not yet been fulfilled. Do you think Jesus has given up on His prayer? I think not.

It is so easy to give up. It is so hard to persevere. The widow in the parable that Jesus told, the woman with the demon-possessed daughter, Abraham, Jesus in the garden, the three Jews cast into the fire, and the mother of Jesus, all had one thing in common. Each one could have said no, or given up at any time. Their stories could have gone like this:

The widow: "Judge, I'm sorry I've been pestering you about this issue. I won't bother you anymore."

The woman from Canaan: "You're right, Jesus, I am a dog, and I shouldn't have asked You. I'll go now."

Abraham: "Lord, You know I love You, but I won't sacrifice my son. That's something I just can't do."

Jesus: "Father, I believe You can make another plan for the salvation of the world. I'm not going to the cross."

Shadrach, Meshach, and Abednego: "King, we made a mistake. We should have worshipped your statue. We're sorry, and from now on we will bow down before it."

Mary: "Son, You're right. It's not Your time to do a miracle. I will sit down and be quiet."

Just one point from the examples above to think about – where would you and I be if Jesus had not gone to the cross?

And I say unto you, Ask, and it shall be given you; seek, and ye shall find; knock, and it shall be opened unto you. For every one that asketh receiveth; and he that seeketh findeth; and to him that knocketh it shall be opened. Luke 11: 9 – 10

The Greek words translated as ask, seek, and knock in these verses should have been translated as keep asking, keep seeking, and keep knocking. In other words, don't give up!

And let us not be weary in well doing: for in due season we shall reap, if we faint not. Galatians 6: 9

God expects us to persevere as we walk with Him. Most often, we don't see or know what the end result will be. That's where faith comes in.

Jacob refused to give up as he was wrestling with the angel, and he reaped the results of his perseverance.

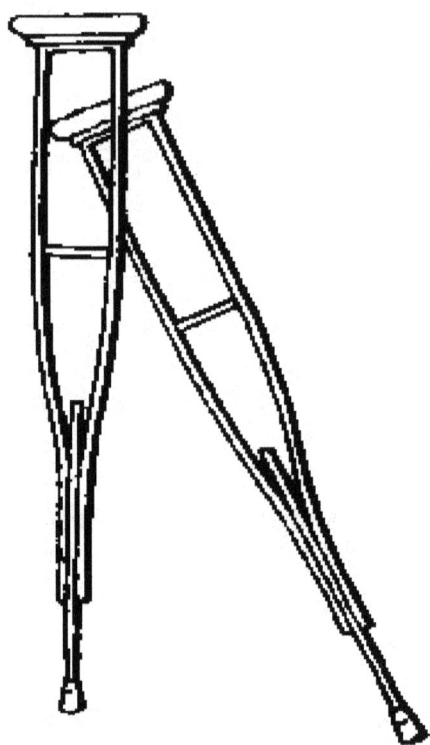

Chapter 8: The break

And Jacob was left alone; and there wrestled a man with him until the breaking of the day. And when he saw that he prevailed not against him, he touched the hollow of his thigh; and the hollow of Jacob's thigh was out of joint, as he wrestled with him. Genesis 32: 24 - 25

If you have ever dislocated your hip, you know how painful it is. When your hip bone is knocked out of its socket, you are left effectively crippled.

This is exactly what happened to Jacob. He was in extreme pain, and yet he refused to give up!

It has been said that God has to break us before He can use us. The psalmist, David, wrote about this experience.

Make me to hear joy and gladness; that the bones which thou hast broken may rejoice. The sacrifices of God are a broken spirit: a broken and a contrite heart, O God, thou wilt not despise. Psalm 51: 8, 17

Have you ever been broken? This happens to us after we have gone our own way, and done our own thing, and everything falls apart. From the human perspective, this is a terrible experience. From God's perspective, it is very necessary.

Allow me to share a poem with you.

Conformed to His image

When every piece has been blackened by the fire
that rains from God,
Removing the protection He once gave,
He beats us with His rod.

And our bloody bits are scattered from the pain
more than one night.
Bleeding out our sins and foolish natures,
We slowly become right.

Whom He loves, He chastens – He has told us this
so many times.
So, then we thank Him for these broken bones,
And He renews our minds.

When every human part is burned beyond ash,
flesh ripped away,
When every drop has been drained out of us,
Our shattered frames like clay –

There's finally room for God to work inside us,
for we are dead.
The carnal man of sin has been replaced
With Jesus Christ instead.

(*From Broken ~ Poems from the Holy Spirit, winner of
the 2021 Illumination Awards Silver Medal for Poetry,
Copyright 2017, Giant Publishing Company*)

I wrote this poem at a time in my life when I had lost
everything that mattered to me. I could see very

clearly the hand of God in my life, His chastening of me, and through it all, His unending love for me.

God loved Jacob. He surely knew that he was a liar and a con man, yet He loved him anyway. I don't know about you, but this gives me great hope.

Jesus saith unto them, Did ye never read in the scriptures, The stone which the builders rejected, the same is become the head of the corner: this is the Lord's doing, and it is marvellous in our eyes? And whosoever shall fall on this stone shall be broken: but on whomsoever it shall fall, it will grind him to powder. Matthew 21: 42, 44

Jesus Christ is the cornerstone of His body, the temple of God, where God Himself resides. When you fall on Him, that is, when you turn your life over to Him, rest assured, you will be broken. Being broken plays itself out in different ways for different people. The end result for all is the death of the carnal man, with his sinful ideas, philosophies and lifestyles, and the birth of Jesus Christ in the inner man.

Falling on Jesus is much preferred over having Him fall on you. If you refuse to turn to Him because of your stubbornness, if you keep telling God that you can manage your own life in your own way, thank you very much, He will eventually fall on you. You will have left Him no choice. And when that happens, you will be crushed to powder.

Jacob knew that he needed God. He was in a desperate situation, about to face his murderous brother (he thought). He was determined to not take another step until God blessed him, even if it meant that he would end up crippled.

Jacob was a wise man. He chose being crippled (brokenness) over being crushed to powder.

You and I also have a choice to make. God is our loving Father, and He has innumerable blessings for us. It is up to us to appropriate these blessings, by refusing to stop asking, seeking, and knocking at His door – by wrestling with Him until He blesses us.

Chapter 9: The blessing

And (the angel) said, Let me go, for the day breaketh. And (Jacob) said, I will not let thee go, except thou bless me. Genesis 32: 26

Jacob was about to meet his brother Esau, who, for all he knew, still wanted to kill him. He was determined to receive a blessing from the angel. Whether this was a guarantee that Esau would not kill him, or that his wives and children would be safe, or something else, we don't know, but he wanted that blessing!

This reminds me of when he stole the blessing from his brother, in chapter 27 of Genesis. His mother planted the idea in his head, and he acted on it. He was determined to have Esau's blessing! Rebekah was also determined.

*...Upon me be thy curse, my son: only obey my voice...*Genesis 27: 13

We have to be so careful of what we say! Rebekah truly did bring a curse upon herself by her careless words. She died without ever seeing her son Jacob again, and never got to see her grandchildren by him. As a mother, I would call that a curse.

This time, there was no stealing involved. Jacob simply refused to let go of the angel. Let's face it, the angel could have ended this wrestling match at any time. Rather than crippling Jacob by knocking his hip out of joint, he could have simply burned him to a crisp in an instant and be done with it. Why engage in a night-long battle with a human being?

As with Abraham, God was testing Jacob. He wanted Jacob to experience what it really means to persevere. God, who is omniscient, knew what Jacob would do before the wrestling match ever started. He wanted Jacob to know, also.

How many times have you given up on something, because it seems that God is not answering you? Speaking for myself, I will say: too many times to count.

And (the angel) said unto him, What is thy name? And he said, Jacob. And he said, Thy name shall be called no more Jacob, but Israel: for as a prince hast thou power with God and with men, and hast prevailed. Genesis 32: 27 – 28

What a blessing! The angel told Jacob that he would no longer be called supplanter, deceiver, or trickster (Jacob), but from that time on he would be called "he who turns the head of God" (Israel).

Praise the Lord – our God is in the business of changing names (natures). He discards our old sin-filled nature, and exchanges it for the spotless nature of His Son.

A divine exchange occurred at Calvary - your sin for His righteousness and your poverty for His provision.

My friend, Jesus is the reason you can be the head and not the tail, above only and not beneath. He is the reason you can be blessed to be a blessing. Put your trust in His presence in your life and what His finished work has accomplished for you! Joseph Prince

This statement by Joseph Prince hits the nail on the head. Jacob had been blessed by God with a new name and a new nature, in order for him to bless others. And he did! Jacob became the father of the twelve tribes of the nation Israel.

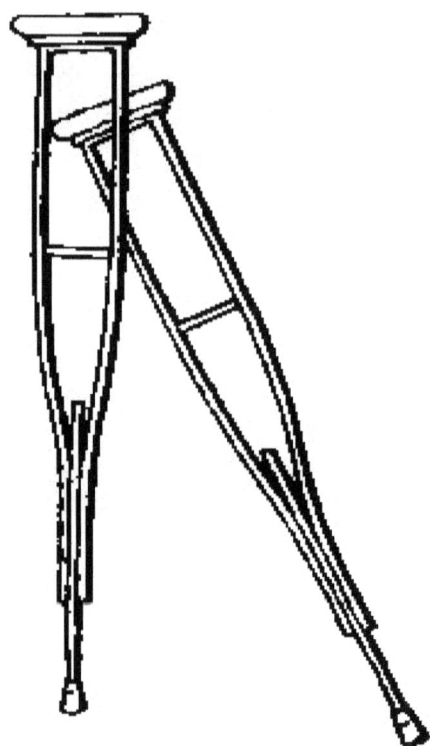

Chapter 10: Limping

*And Jacob asked him, and said, Tell me, I pray thee,
thy name. And he said, Wherefore is it that thou dost
ask after my name? And he blessed him there. And
Jacob called the name of the place Peniel: for I have
seen God face to face, and my life is preserved. And
as he passed over Penuel the sun rose upon him, and
he halted upon his thigh.* Genesis 32: 29 – 31

Jacob wrestled with God, and won. God gave him a
permanent reminder of their wrestling match, which
was a dislocated hip. He also blessed him with a new
name, Israel, and preserved his life.

I think I have an idea of what Jacob was thinking as he
limped along to catch up with his family who had gone
on ahead of him. It was probably something like this:

"It doesn't matter what Esau does to me. I've seen God
face to face. I've received His blessing. He has
blessed me! I'm alive! Nothing else matters now."

*The LORD is on my side; I will not fear: what can
man do unto me?* Psalm 118: 6

The limping former con artist was a changed man.

*And Jacob lifted up his eyes, and looked, and, behold,
Esau came, and with him four hundred men. And he
divided the children unto Leah, and unto Rachel, and
unto the two handmaids. And he put the handmaids
and their children foremost, and Leah and her children
after, and Rachel and Joseph hindermost. And he*

passed over before them, and bowed himself to the ground seven times, until he came near to his brother. And Esau ran to meet him, and embraced him, and fell on his neck, and kissed him: and they wept. Genesis 33: 1 - 4

What a beautiful family reunion. Far from killing him, Esau embraced his brother and wept tears of joy when he saw him. Jacob discovered that Esau had prospered during the years they had been apart from one another. He had his own flocks and herds, servants, wives and children. God had blessed him in spite of the fact that his own brother had stolen his blessing. Esau had, in fact, begged his father to bless him as well as his deceiving brother.

And Esau said unto his father, Hast thou but one blessing, my father? bless me, even me also, O my father. And Esau lifted up his voice, and wept. And Isaac his father answered and said unto him, Behold, thy dwelling shall be the fatness of the earth, and of the dew of heaven from above; And by thy sword shalt thou live, and shalt serve thy brother; and it shall come to pass when thou shalt have the dominion, that thou shalt break his yoke from off thy neck. Genesis 27: 38 - 40

Somewhere along the line, Esau broke free from Jacob's subtle power over him, and became successful on his own.

I wonder if Esau was secretly pleased to see that Jacob now walked with a limp?

52

Chapter 11: Lame for life

Anyone who has wrestled with God is changed profoundly. Jacob certainly was. Receiving God's blessing and a new name did not remove the trouble from his life, however.

In Genesis 34, we read about Dinah, Jacob's daughter, being raped by a man named Shechem. Her brothers, Jacob's eleven sons, were furious that this had happened to their sister. Shechem wanted to marry Dinah, and his father Hamor wanted Jacob to make a deal with him (sound familiar?) whereby Hamor's daughters would marry Jacob's sons, and Jacob's daughters would marry Hamor's sons. Jacob's sons were not about to let that happen. Trickery being a family trait, they used it on Shechem.

And the sons of Jacob answered Shechem and Hamor his father deceitfully, and said, because he had defiled Dinah their sister: And they said unto them, We cannot do this thing, to give our sister to one that is uncircumcised; for that were a reproach unto us: But in this will we consent unto you: If ye will be as we be, that every male of you be circumcised; Then will we give our daughters unto you, and we will take your daughters to us, and we will dwell with you, and we will become one people. But if ye will not hearken unto us, to be circumcised; then will we take our daughter, and we will be gone. Genesis 34: 13 - 17

Hamor had his eye on Jacob's vast herds of animals, so he agreed to be circumcised, along with every man in his city.

Shall not their cattle and their substance and every beast of theirs be ours? only let us consent unto them, and they will dwell with us. Genesis 34: 23

Jacob's sons had no intention of fulfilling their end of the deal. They only wanted revenge against Shechem for raping their sister. They waited three days after all the men had been circumcised to exact their revenge.

And it came to pass on the third day, when they were sore, that two of the sons of Jacob, Simeon and Levi, Dinah's brethren, took each man his sword, and came upon the city boldly, and slew all the males. And they slew Hamor and Shechem his son with the edge of the sword, and took Dinah out of Shechem's house, and went out. The sons of Jacob came upon the slain, and spoiled the city, because they had defiled their sister. They took their sheep, and their oxen, and their asses, and that which was in the city, and that which was in the field, And all their wealth, and all their little ones, and their wives took they captive, and spoiled even all that was in the house. Genesis 34: 25 – 29

Trouble for Jacob. I wonder if sometimes he thought his life would never be free from trouble.

And Jacob said to Simeon and Levi, Ye have troubled me to make me to stink among the inhabitants of the land, among the Canaanites and the Perizzites: and I being few in number, they shall gather themselves together against me, and slay me; and I shall be destroyed, I and my house. And they said, Should he deal with our sister as with an harlot? Genesis 34: 30 - 31

Jacob was more concerned for his reputation in the city of Shechem, than for his daughter's welfare. Nevertheless, his sons' vengeance was extreme.

God never took His eyes off of Jacob. He reminded him of His past blessings and guidance.

And God said unto Jacob, Arise, go up to Bethel, and dwell there: and make there an altar unto God, that appeared unto thee when thou fleddest from the face of Esau thy brother. Genesis 35: 1

This is what is known as a course correction. God had never told Jacob to go to Shechem. When Jacob was still living in his Uncle Laban's house, God told him this:

...Return unto the land of thy fathers, and to thy kindred; and I will be with thee. Genesis 31: 3

What happens when we get off course? In Jacob's case, his daughter was raped, his sons murdered all the men in one city, and Jacob was filled with fear. Therefore, a correction was needed.

Jacob and his family traveled to Bethel, and he built an altar there.

And God appeared unto Jacob again, when he came out of Padanaram, and blessed him. And God said unto him, Thy name is Jacob: thy name shall not be called any more Jacob, but Israel shall be thy name: and he called his name Israel. And God said unto him, I am God Almighty: be fruitful and multiply; a nation and a company of nations shall be of thee, and kings shall come out of thy loins; And the land which I gave Abraham and Isaac, to thee I will give it, and to thy seed after thee will I give the land. And God went up from him in the place where he talked with him. And Jacob set up a pillar in the place where he talked with him, even a pillar of stone: and he poured a drink offering thereon, and he poured oil thereon. And Jacob called the name of the place where God spake with him, Bethel. Genesis 35: 9 – 15

A lot of emphasis is placed on the name of this most recent place where God met Jacob. Bethel means house of God – in other words, "this is where God lives." But note carefully: God told Jacob to go to Bethel and *dwell there* (Genesis 35:1). According to the map, Bethel is about thirty miles from Hebron, where Jacob's father Isaac was living. I believe Jacob was supposed to stay in Bethel.

But he didn't stay there.

And they journeyed from Bethel; and there was but a little way to come to Ephrath: and Rachel travailed, and she had hard labour. Genesis 35: 16

More trouble for Jacob. His beloved wife Rachel went into labor as they were traveling. Would this have happened if they had remained in Bethel? Only God knows.

And it came to pass, when she was in hard labour, that the midwife said unto her, Fear not; thou shalt have this son also. And it came to pass, as her soul was in departing, (for she died) that she called his name Benoni: but his father called him Benjamin. And Rachel died, and was buried in the way to Ephrath, which is Bethlehem. Genesis 35: 17 - 19

Just like that, Jacob's wife was dead. Rachel was the one he fell in love with, at first sight, when she came to the well to water her father's sheep. Rachel was the one he had worked for, for fourteen years. Rachel was the love of his life, and she was dead.

It is one thing to be physically lame, and another thing to be emotionally lame. Jacob was now both.

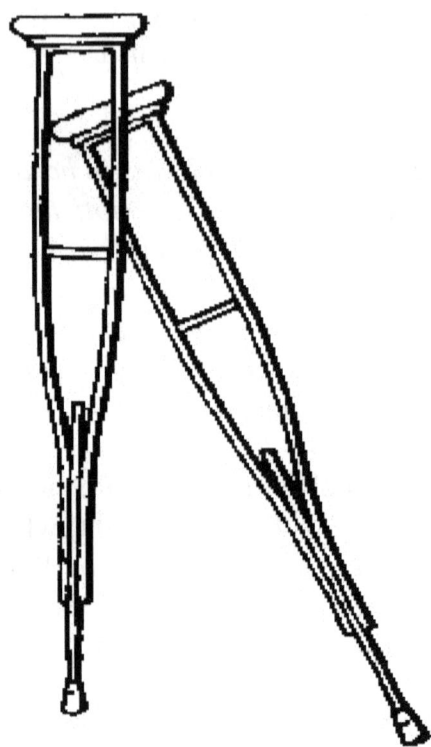

Chapter 12: Walking lame

Jacob placed a pillar on the grave of his beloved wife, Rachel (Genesis 35:20). He then continued on to Hebron, where his father, Isaac was.

The Bible doesn't tell us how long Jacob was with Isaac, but we can surmise that it was a short time. Isaac died sometime after Jacob arrived, and Esau and Jacob buried him (Genesis 35:29).

Now what?

Jacob decided to stay in the place where his father had been living. His twelve sons stayed with him, and they raised animals together.

Jacob's original family, if you remember, was marked by favoritism from the beginning.

And Isaac loved Esau, because he did eat of his venison: but Rebekah loved Jacob. Genesis 25:28

Jacob's later family, with his children, wives and concubines, was no different.

Now Israel loved Joseph more than all his children, because he was the son of his old age: and he made him a coat of many colours. Genesis 37:3

Joseph and Benjamin were the only two of Jacob's sons that were borne by Rachel. She died in childbirth as she was in labor with Benjamin. Technically,

Benjamin should have been called the son of Jacob's old age, but favoritism doesn't always have logic behind it.

Jacob loved Joseph, more than all of his other children. If you come from a large family, you may have seen favoritism firsthand, and you know how painful it can be. Jacob should have known better! Imagine giving one of your children an expensive, beautiful gift, and not giving anything remotely comparable to your other children. This is a recipe for disaster.

Joseph's brother's hated him. They hated him because their father gave him a beautiful coat, which none of them got, and they hated him because God gave him dreams, which none of them received.

Jacob did not use a lot of wisdom in dealing with his children.

And Israel said unto Joseph, Do not thy brethren feed the flock in Shechem? come, and I will send thee unto them. And he said to him, Here am I. And he said to him, Go, I pray thee, see whether it be well with thy brethren, and well with the flocks; and bring me word again. So he sent him out of the vale of Hebron, and he came to Shechem. Genesis 37: 13 -14

Jacob should have known that sending Joseph alone to check on his brothers, who hated him, was probably not a good idea. Either he was ignorant of the situation, or, like many of us parents, he just hoped that his boys would work out their differences in an amicable manner.

That's not what happened. Joseph's brothers saw him coming and plotted to kill him. They tore his beautiful coat off of him, threw him into a pit, and then decided to sell him as a slave to the Ishmeelites. They enriched themselves by twenty pieces of silver – the price of their own brother.

Of course, they would have to come up with a story to tell their father, Jacob, as to why his favorite son never came home.

And they took Joseph's coat, and killed a kid of the goats, and dipped the coat in the blood; And they sent the coat of many colours, and they brought it to their father; and said, This have we found: know now whether it be thy son's coat or no. And he knew it, and said, It is my son's coat; an evil beast hath devoured him; Joseph is without doubt rent in pieces. And Jacob rent his clothes, and put sackcloth upon his loins, and mourned for his son many days. And all his sons and all his daughters rose up to comfort him; but he refused to be comforted; and he said, For I will go down into the grave unto my son mourning. Thus his father wept for him. Genesis 37: 31 - 36

This account highlights the cruelty of Jacob's sons. Their hatred of their brother was so great that they were willing to put their own father through hell, watch him weeping and overcome with grief at the supposed death of his son, and not tell him the truth of what had happened.

This incident added to Jacob's lameness. He spent over twenty years grieving for Joseph.

Have you ever experienced a grief that intense? When we are in deep grief, we feel like the walking dead.

Jacob was already lame physically, from wresting with God. Then his beloved wife, Rachel, died in childbirth. Now, his favorite son was supposedly dead. His emotional lameness had hit a new low.

When life's circumstances have crippled us, we have two choices. We can drop out of life, become bitter and rigid, and refuse to live for God. Some people commit suicide at this point. Or, we can make a determination to continue living for Him, even though we are lame.

Many of us are walking lame. We are doing the best we can, with what we have to work with, limping through life, and praying that God will heal our situations, or take us home.

It is crucial to be honest with God at all times. Don't ever think you can fool God! He knows every thought and feeling you have, before you think and feel. There's no sense in pretending you are "Super-Christian," able to leap tall buildings with a single bound, when in reality you can't get out of bed. He knows you are lame.

I have prayed this prayer many times: "Lord, You know my situation, and You know how much it hurts. You know that most days it's a struggle for me to keep putting one foot in front of the other. But this is where I am! You have the power to change it, but if You don't, I will still live for You and serve You, even though this situation has crippled me. You know what's best for me."

Don't allow bitterness to creep into your life. Bitterness destroys you and everyone around you.

Looking diligently lest any man fail of the grace of God; lest any root of bitterness springing up trouble you, and thereby many be defiled... Hebrews 12:15

I believe some bitterness did creep into Jacob's life. We will read more about this later. But God is so merciful! He had compassion for Jacob, His physically and emotionally lame servant.

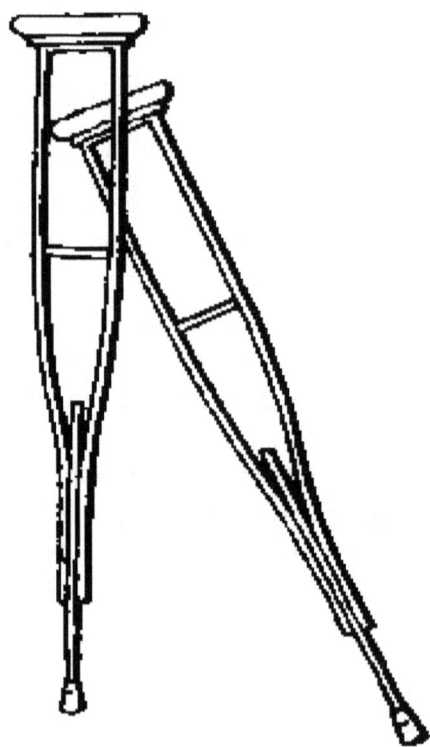

Chapter 13: Living lame

Jacob lived for many years separated from his beloved son, Joseph. He believed that Joseph was dead. He didn't know that God had miraculously preserved Joseph's life, and made him prime minister of Egypt.

One of the reasons Jacob had such a strong connection to Joseph was because of his dreams. God had given Jacob many prophetic dreams, and He had also given dreams to Joseph. The Bible doesn't record that God gave dreams to any other of Jacob's children. In fact, Joseph was promoted to prime minister because he correctly interpreted Pharaoh's dreams about seven years of plenty, followed by seven years of famine. This very fascinating account is told in Genesis 41.

Pharaoh's dreams came true. The land was blessed with abundant production of all crops for a period of seven years. Pharaoh, under Joseph's direction, stored up the excess grain in barns during this seven-year period. No other nation, other than Egypt, did this. So when the years of plenty were over, and the seven years of famine began, all the other nations began to suffer.

Word spread that there was food in Egypt. And Jacob heard about it.

Now when Jacob saw that there was corn in Egypt, Jacob said unto his sons, Why do ye look one upon another? And he said, Behold, I have heard that there is corn in Egypt: get you down thither, and buy for us from thence; that we may live, and not die. Genesis 42: 1 -2

What was going through Jacob's sons' minds? My belief is that they had spent the last twenty-plus years in mental torment over what they had done to their brother Joseph, and what pain and grief they had caused their father. They may even have thought that the famine was God's judgment on them for what they had done. Now their dad was saying, in essence, "Why are you standing around here, staring at each other and doing nothing? Go get us some food."

The way God works is so fascinating, and so far beyond our human comprehension!

For my thoughts are not your thoughts, neither are your ways my ways, saith the LORD. Isaiah 55:8

Jacob's sons could not have known that when they sold their own brother into slavery, God was in fact sending him ahead of them, to prevent their entire family from starving to death. Jacob could not have known that by sending Joseph to check on his brothers that fateful day when they sold him, that Joseph would end up rescuing many nations from famine and death. The boy that he thought was dead and gone was in fact alive and well, and instrumental in reunifying the family, bringing healing, and displaying monumental forgiveness to those who had wronged him.

I love this story; it is my favorite of all the Bible stories.

So, Jacob sent ten of his sons to Egypt to buy food. He kept Benjamin home with him. Benjamin, Jacob's youngest son who was born as his mother was dying, was probably somewhere in his mid-twenties around this time.

And Joseph's ten brethren went down to buy corn in Egypt. But Benjamin, Joseph's brother, Jacob sent not with his brethren; for he said, Lest peradventure mischief befall him. Genesis 42: 3 – 4

Jacob hadn't learned his lesson yet. He was still showing favoritism among his children. Joseph was gone, so Benjamin became his new favorite child. These two were the only children of his beloved wife, Rachel. Therefore, he reasoned, he couldn't allow Benjamin to make the journey to Egypt, because if something happened to him, Jacob would be left without any heirs from Rachel.

We usually can't control who we love. That is to say, we cannot control the emotion of love. Jacob had been tricked by his father-in-law into marrying Leah, a woman he didn't love. Rachel was always the one that he wanted and loved – the one he had worked for, for over twenty years.

And Jacob served seven years for Rachel; and they seemed unto him but a few days, for the love he had to her. Genesis 29: 20

The first seven years was only the beginning of Jacob's servitude for Rachel. Along the way he married Leah, had sons and daughters, was manipulated into working more and more years, and yearned the whole time for Rachel, his true love.

So, from the human perspective, it is natural that Jacob would love Rachel's children more than Leah's, or the children of his two concubines.

But they were all Jacob's children! He seemed to have lost sight of this because of his extraordinary love for Rachel.

As I stated before, favoritism was the norm in Jacob's family.

In Genesis 42, we read the beautiful and fascinating story of how Joseph met his brothers again in Egypt, how he sent them home to their father with plenty of food and money, and how he had a bit of fun (my opinion) in toying with them. Among other things, Joseph told his brothers that they needed to bring their youngest brother with them the next time they came, and he held Simeon hostage as a guarantee that they would come back! He had recognized them immediately, but they hadn't recognized him.

We also see Jacob, an old man, and all of his fears and anxieties once again coming to the surface.

And they came unto Jacob their father unto the land of Canaan, and told him all that befell unto them; saying, The man, who is the lord of the land, spake roughly to

us… (and said) bring your youngest brother unto me…
Genesis 42: 29 – 30a, 34a

Jacob's sons were truly in between a rock and a hard place. They were now convinced that God was punishing them because of what they'd done to Joseph (verses 21 and 22).

And Jacob their father said unto them, Me have ye bereaved of my children: Joseph is not, and Simeon is not, and ye will take Benjamin away: all these things are against me. And Reuben spake unto his father, saying, Slay my two sons, if I bring him not to thee: deliver him into my hand, and I will bring him to thee again. And he said, My son shall not go down with you; for his brother is dead, and he is left alone: if mischief befall him by the way in the which ye go, then shall ye bring down my gray hairs with sorrow to the grave. Genesis 42: 36 – 38

Jacob was desperately trying to hold onto Benjamin, his last reminder of Rachel. But God had other plans.

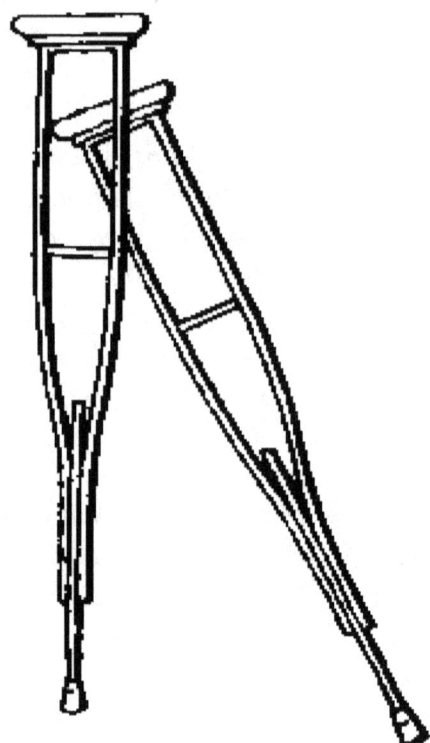

Chapter 14: Blessed for life

After the family had eaten all the food they brought back from Egypt, Jacob told his sons to go back and get more. Judah reminded his father that the prime minister – his own brother, although he didn't know it at the time – had told them to not bother coming back unless they brought Benjamin with them.

Another family wrestling match ensued.

If thou wilt send our brother with us, we will go down and buy thee food: But if thou wilt not send him, we will not go down: for the man said unto us, Ye shall not see my face, except your brother be with you. And Israel said, Wherefore dealt ye so ill with me, as to tell the man whether ye had yet a brother? And they said, The man asked us straitly of our state, and of our kindred, saying, Is your father yet alive? have ye another brother? and we told him according to the tenor of these words: could we certainly know that he would say, Bring your brother down? And Judah said unto Israel his father, Send the lad with me, and we will arise and go; that we may live, and not die, both we, and thou, and also our little ones. I will be surety for him; of my hand shalt thou require him: if I bring him not unto thee, and set him before thee, then let me bear the blame for ever: For except we had lingered, surely now we had returned this second time. And their father Israel said unto them, If it must be so now, do this; take of the best fruits in the land in your vessels, and carry down the man a present, a little balm, and a little honey, spices, and myrrh, nuts, and almonds: And take double money in your hand; and the money that was brought again in the mouth of your sacks, carry it again in your hand; peradventure it was an oversight: Take also your brother, and arise, go again unto the man: And God Almighty give you mercy before the man, that he may send away your other brother, and Benjamin. If I be bereaved of my children, I am bereaved. Genesis 43: 4 - 14

You can almost hear the irritation in Jacob's voice. "You stupid boys! Why did you tell him you had another brother? Can't you keep your mouths shut? Why did you spill all our family business to this stranger?"

You can also hear the resignation in his voice, as he tells his sons to go ahead and take Benjamin with them, as there seems to be no other way to get food.

"All right, sons, if it has to be this way, take the man a gift. Maybe that will soften him up a little. And take enough money for this time and last time. Take Benjamin, too! If I lose another son, so be it."

Once again, I feel sorry for Jacob.

Benjamin went with his brothers to Egypt. Joseph had a bit more fun toying with all of them. I have never quite understood this, but perhaps it was necessary in order for them to fully realize that Joseph had the power to destroy all of them, yet chose not to use it.

Joseph finally told his brothers who he was (Genesis 45:1). The wheels of family reunification were now set in motion.

Haste ye, and go up to my father, and say unto him, Thus saith thy son Joseph, God hath made me lord of all Egypt: come down unto me, tarry not: And thou shalt dwell in the land of Goshen, and thou shalt be near unto me, thou, and thy children, and thy children's children, and thy flocks, and thy herds, and all that thou hast: And there will I nourish thee; for yet there are five years of famine; lest thou, and thy household, and all that thou hast, come to poverty. And, behold, your eyes see, and the eyes of my brother Benjamin, that it is my mouth that speaketh unto you. And ye shall tell my father of all my glory in Egypt, and of all that ye have seen; and ye shall haste and bring down my father hither. Genesis 45: 9 - 13

We can only imagine what Joseph's brothers felt when they realized who he was. Joseph immediately sent them back to fetch their father. I think he felt a sense of urgency, because he knew Jacob was old, and probably didn't have much time left. He wanted to see him as soon as possible.

So he sent his brethren away, and they departed: and he said unto them, See that ye fall not out by the way. And they went up out of Egypt, and came into the land of Canaan unto Jacob their father, And told him, saying, Joseph is yet alive, and he is governor over all the land of Egypt. And Jacob's heart fainted, for he believed them not. And they told him all the words of

Joseph, which he had said unto them: and when he saw the wagons which Joseph had sent to carry him, the spirit of Jacob their father revived: And Israel said, It is enough; Joseph my son is yet alive: I will go and see him before I die. Genesis 45: 24 - 28

Jacob was no fool. At some point he must have figured out that the story his sons had told him about finding Joseph's coat covered with blood, was a flat-out lie. Scripture doesn't tell us if the brothers ever confessed to Jacob what they had done, although it is implied in Genesis 50: 16 – 17.

I think none of that mattered to Jacob at this point. His son, who he'd thought for years was dead, was very much alive, and now he was finally going to see him once again.

Chapter 15: Generational blessings

God once again visited Jacob and spoke to him.

And Israel took his journey with all that he had, and came to Beersheba, and offered sacrifices unto the God of his father Isaac. And God spake unto Israel in the visions of the night, and said, Jacob, Jacob. And he said, Here am I. And he said, I am God, the God of thy father: fear not to go down into Egypt; for I will there make of thee a great nation: I will go down with thee into Egypt; and I will also surely bring thee up again: and Joseph shall put his hand upon thine eyes. And Jacob rose up from Beersheba: and the sons of Israel carried Jacob their father, and their little ones, and their wives, in the wagons which Pharaoh had sent to carry him. And they took their cattle, and their goods, which they had gotten in the land of Canaan, and came into Egypt, Jacob, and all his seed with him: His sons, and his sons' sons with him, his daughters, and his sons' daughters, and all his seed brought he with him into Egypt. Genesis 46: 1-7

There is a lot to think about in these verses. As soon as Jacob realized that Joseph was, in fact, alive and living in Egypt, he didn't waste any time. He packed up his extended family and everything he owned, and headed to Egypt. God spoke to him in the night, and told him that He was going to bless him by making him a great nation.

It's very interesting to me that Almighty God, who wrestled with Jacob and gave him a new name, Israel, still addressed him with his previous name when He called out to him in the night. I have heard some preachers say that Jacob is referred to as Jacob when he is acting like Jacob – lying, tricking, being deceitful. He is referred to as Israel when he is acting as Israel – a prince of God, one who turns God's head. This may be true; I don't know. But I don't see any evidence of deceit in the verses above.

Jacob and his family arrived in Egypt, and Joseph came out to meet them.

And Joseph made ready his chariot, and went up to meet Israel his father, to Goshen, and presented himself unto him; and he fell on his neck, and wept on his neck a good while. And Israel said unto Joseph, Now let me die, since I have seen thy face, because thou art yet alive. Genesis 46: 29 - 30

Jacob now had everything he wanted. He felt that he could die in peace, having seen Joseph alive and well. But God was not about to let Jacob die at this time.

And Joseph brought in Jacob his father, and set him before Pharaoh: and Jacob blessed Pharaoh. And Pharaoh said unto Jacob, How old art thou? And Jacob said unto Pharaoh, The days of the years of my pilgrimage are an hundred and thirty years: few and evil have the days of the years of my life been, and have not attained unto the days of the years of the life of my fathers in the days of their pilgrimage. And Jacob blessed Pharaoh, and went out from before Pharaoh. Genesis 47: 7 - 10

Remember earlier when I stated that some bitterness had crept into Jacob's life? "Few and evil have the days of the years of my life been..." Those sound like the words of a bitter man. But we can't really blame Jacob for feeling bitter.

Please don't misunderstand – bitterness is a sin, and we need to fight against it (Hebrews 12:15). I am simply saying that most of us can relate to Jacob's attitude!

In spite of the lies he had told and the trickery he had committed, Jacob was a chosen man of God. Even Pharaoh recognized this. He allowed Jacob to bless him. Pharaoh, a pagan ruler who no doubt worshipped carved images, recognized that the one true God had His hand on Jacob, and wanted Jacob to bless him.

And Israel dwelt in the land of Egypt, in the country of Goshen; and they had possessions therein, and grew, and multiplied exceedingly. And Jacob lived in the land of Egypt seventeen years: so the whole age of Jacob was an hundred forty and seven years. And the time drew nigh that Israel must die: and he called his son Joseph, and said unto him, If now I have found grace in thy sight, put, I pray thee, thy hand under my thigh, and deal kindly and truly with me; bury me not, I pray thee, in Egypt: But I will lie with my fathers, and thou shalt carry me out of Egypt, and bury me in their buryingplace. And he said, I will do as thou hast said. And he said, Swear unto me. And he sware unto

him. And Israel bowed himself upon the bed's head.
Genesis 47: 27 – 31

God, in His great mercy, had allowed Jacob to travel to Egypt, to see his son before he died. This was not just for Jacob's benefit; it was for the benefit of his entire family. As Jacob was on his deathbed, Joseph came to see him one final time, and he brought Manasseh and Ephraim, his two sons, with him.

And Jacob said unto Joseph, God Almighty appeared unto me at Luz in the land of Canaan, and blessed me, And said unto me, Behold, I will make thee fruitful, and multiply thee, and I will make of thee a multitude of people; and will give this land to thy seed after thee for an everlasting possession. Genesis 48: 3 – 4

What follows is a beautiful blessing. Jacob blessed Manasseh and Ephraim, and blessed all twelve of his sons. Like his father Isaac, Jacob gave the firstborn's blessing to Joseph's younger son, but unlike Isaac, this was done intentionally.

And Joseph said unto his father, Not so, my father: for this is the firstborn; put thy right hand upon his head. And his father refused, and said, I know it, my son, I know it: he also shall become a people, and he also shall be great: but truly his younger brother shall be greater than he, and his seed shall become a multitude of nations. And he blessed them that day, saying, In thee shall Israel bless, saying, God make thee as Ephraim and as Manasseh: and he set Ephraim before Manasseh. And Israel said unto Joseph, Behold, I die:

but God shall be with you, and bring you again unto the land of your fathers. Genesis 48: 18 - 21

Jacob then called all twelve of his sons, and pronounced a blessing over them all.

...and this is it that their father spake unto them, and blessed them; every one according to his blessing he blessed them. And he charged them, and said unto them, I am to be gathered unto my people: bury me with my fathers in the cave that is in the field of Ephron the Hittite, In the cave that is in the field of Machpelah, which is before Mamre, in the land of Canaan, which Abraham bought with the field of Ephron the Hittite for a possession of a buryingplace. There they buried Abraham and Sarah his wife; there they buried Isaac and Rebekah his wife; and there I buried Leah. The purchase of the field and of the cave that is therein was from the children of Heth. And when Jacob had made an end of commanding his sons, he gathered up his feet into the bed, and yielded up the ghost, and was gathered unto his people. Genesis 49: 28b – 33

That is the end of Jacob's life on earth, but just the beginning of his generational blessings.

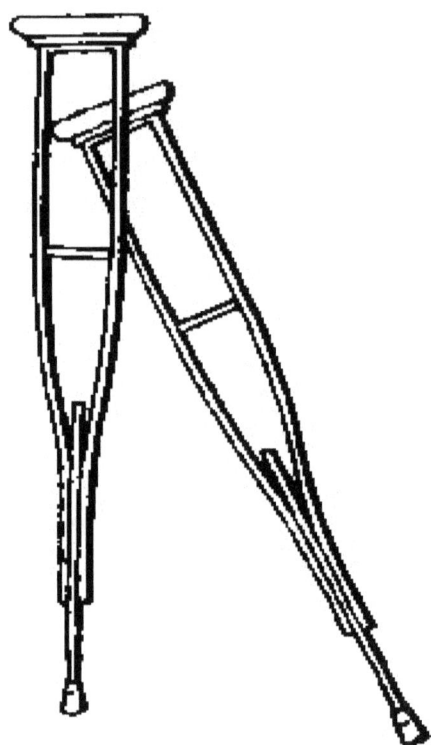

Chapter 16: Will you wrestle?

Are you willing to wrestle with God? Are you willing to do whatever it takes to receive your blessing?

Let's take a moment to review the life of Jacob.

1. He was a liar and a con man.
2. He saw the error of his ways.
3. He asked God to bless him, and wouldn't take no for an answer.
4. He wrestled with God until God crippled him.
5. God gave him a new name and blessings that lasted for generations.
6. While waiting for the generational blessings, he endured extreme heartache.
7. He emerged victorious in the end, his family was reunited, and he died at a ripe old age, blessed and comforted.

Is this a life pattern that you want to duplicate?

I think most of us would answer: No. Sure, we would like to see the error of our ways, would gladly receive a new name, happily take blessings and comfort, and be satisfied to die at a ripe old age. But the rest of the things on that list? Nobody wants those.

And yet, this is exactly what God expects of us.

It's a good idea to take periodic stock of ourselves and our lives. When you see a problem (Jacob saw that he was a liar), repent of it, ask God to forgive you, and ask Him to help you not to sin again (John 8:11).

Now, ask God for His blessings in your life. I grew up thinking that somehow it was wrong to ask God for anything. I felt that it was greedy, or selfish. But it's not!

Give us this day our daily bread. Matthew 6:11

If Jesus taught us to pray and ask God for our daily bread, it is certainly not a sin to do so. Everything that we have comes from God; it is absolutely foolish to think that you have provided anything for yourself.

But thou shalt remember the LORD thy God: for it is he that giveth thee power to get wealth, that he may establish his covenant which he sware unto thy fathers, as it is this day. Deuteronomy 8:18

Whatever money I have, the Lord gave it to me. When I use the money he gave me to buy my daily bread, or put gas in my car, or anything else, I remember that He is the one who provided it to me.

If ye then, being evil, know how to give good gifts unto your children: how much more shall your heavenly Father give the Holy Spirit to them that ask him? Luke 11:13

In additional to material blessings, I ask God for many spiritual blessings. The verse above states that if we ask Him for the Holy Spirit, He will give Him to us.

Some people believe that once you are born again, you automatically have the Holy Spirit, and you are complete. Personally, I ask for the Holy Spirit every day – to lead me, to empower me, to strengthen me, to encourage me, and to comfort me. I need Him. If we have to eat physical bread daily to stay alive, we certainly need to get our daily portion of spiritual food to stay spiritually alive.

I ask God for wisdom every day. Wisdom is a spiritual blessing. The consequences of living a life without wisdom are severe. That's why I ask Him for it.

Ask God for whatever blessings you want. He wants to bless us! God in His mercy blesses all humanity with what are known as common blessings. In other words, you have a planet to live on, sunshine and air to breathe, regardless of whether you ask for these things or not. He gives them to believer and unbeliever alike. But His blessings are innumerable! Ask Him to bless you. You won't be blessed if you don't ask. But remember this:

Ye lust, and have not: ye kill, and desire to have, and cannot obtain: ye fight and war, yet ye have not, because ye ask not. Ye ask, and receive not, because ye ask amiss, that ye may consume it upon your lusts.
James 4: 2 – 3

You won't be blessed if you don't ask, and you also won't be blessed if you ask for unnecessary things that you want just because you are greedy. (This verse is why I was hesitant to ask for anything; I thought I was being greedy if I asked for a new pair of shoes, if my old ones had holes in them!)

If you have a good car that runs well, you don't need to ask for another car. If you are a minister of the gospel who flies all over the world preaching, and you are at the mercy of United Airlines and their flight delays, cancellations, and lost luggage, you had better be asking God for a private jet, and soon!

I hope you can see the difference.

Many times, I have asked God for a huge amount of money. Why? So I can give it to people that I know who are struggling financially. So far, I have not received it. Perhaps God knows that I would not handle it wisely! But I still ask Him, and will continue.

Ask, and it shall be given you; seek, and ye shall find; knock, and it shall be opened unto you: For every one that asketh receiveth; and he that seeketh findeth; and to him that knocketh it shall be opened. Matthew 7: 7 – 8

As I stated in Chapter 7, the words ask, seek and knock should have been translated as keep asking, keep seeking, keep knocking. If we want to receive God's blessings, we simply must not give up.

There is an exception to this. If you ask for something, and God says no, please don't keep asking Him.

Why? Because God's principles remain the same, whether you and I are right or wrong. If we ask for the right thing and don't give up, He will give it to us. And if we ask for the wrong thing and don't give up, He will give it to us. If you are determined to have your own way, and refuse to listen to the still, small voice of the Holy Spirit, God will give you what you asked for, and it will be disaster and destruction for you.

Look at the prodigal son (Luke 15: 11 – 32). That boy was determined to have his own way. His father gave him what he asked for. He ended up starving, in rags, and sleeping in a pig pen.

You will know if God has said no to your request. There is actually a simple way to know. In my own life, I had once asked God for something that was a "gray area" in the Christian life. I couldn't actually say that it was a sin, but I also couldn't really say for certain that it wasn't a sin, either. But I really wanted it! I almost became obsessed by it. I finally asked God to take away my desire for it, if it was something He didn't want me to have. Literally overnight, the desire disappeared. That's how I knew His answer was no.

This is what is meant by those beautiful words in the twenty-third Psalm:

He restoreth my soul: he leadeth me in the paths of righteousness for his name's sake. Psalm 23:3

I don't know how to lead myself! That's why God must lead me.

Are you willing to let God cripple you, in order to bless you?

But he was wounded for our transgressions, he was bruised for our iniquities: the chastisement of our peace was upon him; and with his stripes we are healed. Isaiah 53:5

Jesus Christ was crippled on the cross, in order to facilitate the greatest blessing the world has ever known. If He was willing, you and I must be willing as well.

The process of being crippled is not easy! It is extremely painful. It is also hard to understand.

Everything that I want, or think I want, must be laid aside in order for God to work through me. This destroys the human, fleshly nature that we all have. This cripples us, humanly speaking.

After Jacob was crippled, even though he walked with a limp, he was blessed!

Next, do you want a new name?

In our modern society, it's fairly easy to change one's name. You just complete some paperwork, go to court, and get a new name. Having a new legal name does nothing to change your character, however. When God changes your name, He gives you a new nature. The word name means nature. This is why we pray "in Jesus' name."

I want a new nature! I am not at all satisfied with my old, sinful, fleshly, carnal human nature. In fact, I am quite disgusted by it. I want God's nature.

Jacob's grandfather, Abram, also had received a new name from God.

Neither shall thy name any more be called Abram, but thy name shall be Abraham; for a father of many nations have I made thee. Genesis 17:5

The name Abram means high father, and the name Abraham means father of many. God knew what He was doing when He changed Abram's name. Abraham is known world-wide as the father of the Jewish people, a nation which the scripture describes as being more than the sand of the sea in number (Genesis 22:17).

Jacob's grandmother, Sarai, also got a new name.

And God said unto Abraham, As for Sarai thy wife, thou shalt not call her name Sarai, but Sarah shall her name be. Genesis 17:15

Sarai, a "contentious person," became Sarah, "a princess." Only God can do that!

Jesus also gave out a new name.

And Simon Peter answered and said, Thou art the Christ, the Son of the living God. And Jesus answered and said unto him, Blessed art thou, Simon Barjona: for flesh and blood hath not revealed it unto thee, but my Father which is in heaven. And I say also unto thee, That thou art Peter, and upon this rock I will build my church; and the gates of hell shall not prevail against it. Matthew 16: 16 – 18

Simon means to listen or to hear. Peter means rock. (Simon Barjona means Simon, the son of Jona.) Like Jacob, Peter was sometimes referred to by his old name, Simon, and sometimes referred to by his new name, Peter. Peter was the first one who publicly stated that Jesus was the Messiah. This statement, which all believers must make publicly at some point in their lives, is the rock that the church is built upon. The church is not built upon Peter, the human being.

For other foundation can no man lay than that is laid, which is Jesus Christ. 1 Corinthians 3:11

Saul of Tarsus, who hated and persecuted Christians, had a dramatic encounter with Jesus Christ as he was journeying to Damascus. The Bible doesn't record exactly when or how Saul got his new name, but we know he did.

Then Saul, (who also is called Paul,) filled with the Holy Ghost, set his eyes on him. Acts 13:9

We can conclude that somewhere along the line, Jesus gave Saul his new name, Paul.

*Behold, I make all things new...*Revelation 21: 5b

I don't know about you, but I am so grateful to God that He is in the business of making us new. The past is gone when you are in Jesus Christ. He has a glorious future awaiting you and me.

Are you willing to endure heartache as you are waiting for your blessings?

Whether you are willing or not, if you are a follower of Jesus Christ, you will suffer heartache. It is part of being a Christian.

Are they ministers of Christ? (I speak as a fool) I am more; in labours more abundant, in stripes above measure, in prisons more frequent, in deaths oft. Of the Jews five times received I forty stripes save one. Thrice was I beaten with rods, once was I stoned, thrice I suffered shipwreck, a night and a day I have been in the deep; In journeyings often, in perils of waters, in perils of robbers, in perils by mine own countrymen, in perils by the heathen, in perils in the city, in perils in the wilderness, in perils in the sea, in perils among false brethren; In weariness and painfulness, in watchings often, in hunger and thirst, in fastings often, in cold and nakedness. 2 Corinthians 11: 23 - 27

This is just one man's account! The apostle Paul probably suffered more than any other follower of Christ, but history and the Bible record endless accounts of Christians who were imprisoned, beaten, tortured, boiled in oil and burned at the stake, because they refused to denounce Christ. These things are still going on today. I try to remind myself of this, whenever I feel that my life is too hard!

With every privilege comes a corresponding responsibility. As Christians, if we want the blessings of God, we must be willing to pay the price for them. Wrestling with God comes at great personal human cost, but the blessings are beyond human calculation.

But as it is written, Eye hath not seen, nor ear heard, neither have entered into the heart of man, the things which God hath prepared for them that love him. 1 Corinthians 2:9

Will you wrestle? Will you grab ahold of God, and not let Him go until He blesses you? I pray that you will.

Jacob wrestled with God, was crippled by God, received God's blessing and a new name, and changed the world forever.

Chapter 17: God's example to us

How is it possible for a human being to wrestle with God, to refuse to let go of Him, to ask Him for a blessing and not stop asking until it is received?

It is possible, because God Himself has shown us how, by His own example.

And, behold, I am with thee, and will keep thee in all places whither thou goest, and will bring thee again into this land; for I will not leave thee, until I have done that which I have spoken to thee of.   Genesis 28: 15

God will not leave us. He will do what He has said He will do.

...for he hath said, I will never leave thee, nor forsake thee. Hebrews 13:5b

God will not let go of us until He has finished His work in each one of us. His work is different for every person.

*Being confident of this very thing, that he which hath begun a good work in   you   will perform it until the day of Jesus Christ...*Philippians 1: 6

When God makes a promise to man, He never lets go of it.

And I will establish my covenant with you, neither shall all flesh be cut off any more by the waters of a flood; neither shall there any more be a flood to destroy the earth. And God said, This is the token of the covenant which I make between me and you and every living creature that is with you, for perpetual generations: I do set my bow in the cloud, and it shall be for a token of a covenant between me and the earth. Genesis 9: 11 – 13

God made a covenant with mankind, that He would never again flood the entire earth. This covenant stands, whether we sin or don't sin, whether we follow Him or don't follow Him.

Behold, I have graven thee upon the palms of my hands; thy walls are continually before me. Isaiah 49:16

God is holding onto you and me so tightly that our image has been imprinted onto the palms of His hands. He will not let go!

And I set my tabernacle among you: and my soul shall not abhor you. And I will walk among you, and will be your God, and ye shall be my people. Leviticus 26: 11 – 12

What is God's tabernacle? It's you and I.

*Howbeit the most High dwelleth not in temples made with hands; as saith the prophet...*Acts 7: 48

What? know ye not that your body is the temple of the Holy Ghost which is in you, which ye have of God, and ye are not your own? 1 Corinthians 6: 19

A minister of the sanctuary, and of the true tabernacle, which the Lord pitched, and not man. Hebrews 8: 2

*But Christ being come an high priest of good things to come, by a greater and more perfect tabernacle, not made with hands, that is to say, not of this building...*Hebrews 9: 11

Yea, I think it meet, as long as I am in this tabernacle, to stir you up by putting you in remembrance; Knowing that shortly I must put off this my tabernacle, even as our Lord Jesus Christ hath shewed me. 2 Peter 1: 13 – 4

God's tabernacle is His people, and He is within us and among us. He cannot be separated from us.

Remember Jesus' prayer in John chapter 17.

That they all may be one; as thou, Father, art in me, and I in thee, that they also may be one in us: that the world may believe that thou hast sent me. John 17: 21

Jesus is clinging to the Father and His promises to His people. Jesus hasn't given up on what He asked His Father to do, two thousand years ago. Don't you and I give up on what we have asked God to do, either. Wrestle with Him until He blesses you!

Always remember this: God clings to us so tightly. He never leaves us. He finishes the work He has started in us. He has made us His tabernacle. Therefore, we can cling to Him and never let go until He blesses us. He has set the example for us! He has done it, and we can do it, too.

It is my prayer that you will wrestle with Almighty God, and not give up until He blesses you.

Please visit our website for more resources:

www.giantpublishingcompany.com

And he spake a parable unto them to this end, that
*men ought always to pray, and not to faint...*Luke 18:1

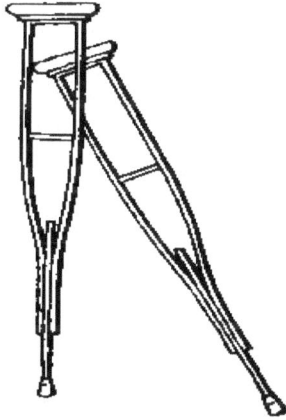

www.ingramcontent.com/pod-product-compliance
Lightning Source LLC
Chambersburg PA
CBHW070056100426
42740CB00013B/2849